on **Going to Court**

Alexandra Conroy Harris

BAAF Cymru
7 Cleeve House
Lambourne Crescent
Cardiff
CF14 5GP

Published by
**British Association for Adoption & Fostering
(BAAF)**
Saffron House
6–10 Kirby Street
London EC1N 8TS
www.baaf.org.uk

Charity registration 275689 (England and Wales)
and SC039337 (Scotland)

British Library Cataloguing in Publication Data
A catalogue record for this book is available from the British Library

ISBN 978 1 910039 16 8

Project management by Jo Francis, Publications Department, BAAF
Designed by Helen Joubert Designs
Typeset by Fravashi Aga
Printed in Great Britain by T J International Ltd

Trade distribution by Turnaround Publisher Services, Unit 3,
Olympia Trading Estate, Coburg Road, London N22 6TZ

BAAF is the leading UK-wide membership organisation for all those
concerned with adoption, fostering and child care issues.

Contents

This series

Ten Top Tips on Going to Court is the twelfth title in BAAF's *Ten Top Tips* series. This series tackles some fundamental issues in the area of adoption and fostering with the aim of presenting them in a quick reference format. Previous titles are:

- *Ten Top Tips for Placing Children*, by Hedi Argent
- *Ten Top Tips for Managing Contact*, by Henrietta Bond
- *Ten Top Tips for Finding Families*, by Jennifer Cousins
- *Ten Top Tips for Placing Siblings*, by Hedi Argent
- *Ten Top Tips for Preparing Care Leavers*, by Henrietta Bond
- *Ten Top Tips for Making Introductions*, by Lindsey Dunbar
- *Ten Top Tips for Supporting Kinship Placements*, by Hedi Argent
- *Ten Top Tips for Supporting Adopters*, by Jeanne Kaniuk with Eileen Fursland
- *Ten Top Tips for Identifying Neglect*, by Pat Beesley
- *Ten Top Tips for Making Matches*, by Jennifer Cousins
- *Ten Top Tips for Supporting Education*, by Eileen Fursland with Kate Cairns and Chris Stanway

Details are available on www.baaf.org.uk.

Note about the author

Alexandra Conroy Harris

Alexandra Conroy Harris was called to the Bar in 1989. She practised as a self-employed barrister in London and the South East, representing local authorities, children and parents in public and private law proceedings. She was employed for nine years as a social services lawyer for a London borough, representing the borough in cases involving children and vulnerable adults and providing training, support and advice to local authority social workers.

Since 2008, she has been employed as the Legal Consultant to BAAF, providing advice to everyone involved in adoption and fostering. She is also the Legal Adviser to the IRM Cymru.

Acknowledgements

Thanks to Marjorie Morrison, Jeffrey Coleman and Mary Francis, who read and commented on an early draft of this book, and to Maureen Floyd and Michael Conroy Harris for their comments and suggestions.

Introduction

In November 2008, details of the circumstances surrounding the death a year earlier of Peter Connelly, known as Baby P, were published. Peter was a 17-month-old child who was known to children's services and other bodies, but suffered over 50 injuries in the eight months before his death in August 2007. His mother, her boyfriend and a lodger were convicted of causing or allowing his death. The case led to a widespread review of child protection and the number of applications for care orders in England and Wales rose from 1,148 in the April–June quarter of 2008 to 2,087 in the same quarter of 2009 (CAFCASS, 2014).

The number of applications has remained high since 2008 and in January–March 2014, 2,678 care cases were started by local authorities in England and Wales. This has meant that more and more social workers are needing to become involved in preparing and presenting cases to court. This guide is intended to support social workers who are new to court proceedings, whether they are bringing a case themselves or attending court to give evidence, and to increase their confidence in facing what can sometimes appear a daunting prospect – their day in court.

This guide focuses primarily on the court procedures of England and Wales, although similarities and differences between the processes in England and Wales and Northern Ireland are identified and basic court skills are common to all jurisdictions.*

---

* Court procedures differ considerably in Scotland, and will be addressed in a forthcoming Ten Top Tips title from BAAF.

1

TIP 1

Only go to court if absolutely necessary

Court proceedings can be a powerful tool in effecting positive change for a child at risk in their family situation, but should be used only as a last resort. Every effort should be made to protect the child by negotiation and agreement with the parents and wider family before legal proceedings are contemplated. This chapter looks at alternative actions that should be considered before deciding to go to court.

However, there are always going to be cases where working with the family is not enough; where the child is placed in an immediately dangerous situation; where the parents are unwilling or unable to make the changes that will allow them to parent their child adequately; or where there is nothing that can be done to protect the child from the risk of significant harm. In those cases, when that point is reached, the only option will be to start proceedings, usually with the intention of removing the child from the family.

Going to court is not an easy thing to do. It requires the investment of significant resources, social work time and lawyers' time. It creates an adversarial relationship with a family you may have been trying to work with for months and heightens tension for the child whom you are trying to protect. Starting proceedings can end all co-operation from the family and force the local authority into a position where the child has to be removed from home.

On the other hand, there can be advantages for the parents of making the decision to go to court. In England and Wales, the local authority has to issue a pre-proceedings letter before applying to court. This is a trigger for the Legal Services Commission to allow access to funding for independent legal advice, which is not available while a child is subject only to a child protection plan. This letter has to set out clearly the difficulties that the local authority has identified and what the family has to do to avoid proceedings. It can be a wake-up call for a family, prompting a realisation of just how seriously the local authority is viewing the situation, and how close they may be to losing their child.

Consider the Welfare Checklist

The Children Act 1989 s.1 (England and Wales) and the Children (Northern Ireland) Order 1995 s.3 list the matters that the court will take into account when considering whether or not to make an order in respect of a child. The statutes in all parts of the UK are based on the principle that the child's welfare shall be the court's 'paramount consideration' (s.1(1) Children Act 1989, s.3(1) Children (Northern Ireland) Order 1995).

Welfare Checklist

(a)   the ascertainable wishes and feelings of the child concerned (considered in the light of his age and understanding);

(b)   his physical, emotional and educational needs;

(c)   the likely effect on him of any change in his circumstances;

(d) his age, sex, background and any characteristics of his which the court considers relevant;

(e) any harm which he has suffered or is at risk of suffering;

(f) how capable each of his parents, and any other person in relation to whom the court considers the question to be relevant, is of meeting his needs;

(g) the range of powers available to the court under this Act in the proceedings in question.

Children Act 1989 s.1(3)

In deciding whether or not an application should be made to the court, the same questions should be asked by the local authority.

Can the child's welfare be protected by consent?

If the child's parents accept some or all of the local authority's concerns, they may be willing to agree to measures that will protect the child without the need to issue proceedings. If one member of the family is the cause of concern, the child's parents may agree to that family member leaving the home; if the physical conditions of the child's care are inadequate, they may accept help to change those conditions.

Parents may even agree to the child being removed from the home, especially if the child is moved to a relative or for a short fixed term (for example, to allow a parent to undertake treatment for substance misuse). However, such agreement can only be accepted where the parents are fully informed of the options available to them and have access to appropriate advice before consenting to the child being removed.

CASE STUDY

A mother had been through three sets of care proceedings and in each case her child had been removed from her care and placed for adoption. Pre-birth assessments concluded that she would be unable to care for her fourth child and the plan was for the baby to be removed immediately after birth. The mother had learning difficulties and, on the day of the child's birth, had to make decisions about surgery for herself, about using morphine to which she thought she was allergic, and whether to consent to the baby's placement in care. Initially she refused to consent. After taking morphine, but without having spoken to her solicitor, she later agreed to the baby being accommodated. The High Court gave guidance on the making of agreements for the accommodation of children, including the social worker's personal responsibility to ensure that the mother had capacity to consent and understood fully the options available to her. Where there was doubt about this, it would be fairer to make an application to the court.

In this case, the child could have remained in hospital with the mother and a court would not have ordered immediate removal. The local authority accepted that it had breached the mother's and child's right to a family life and agreed to pay compensation.

Re CA (A Baby)[2012] EWHC 2190(Fam)

Could a Family Group Conference find either short- or long-term solutions for the child?

Parents may well have been unwilling or unable to disclose the full extent of their difficulties to their families. Holding a Family Group Conference (FGC) enables the child's relatives to understand the family situation and that the child is at real risk of being taken into care. Properly done, it can give the family a chance to put in place their own protective network to allow the child to remain safely at home or to look after him. Another family member may be able to look after the child in the short term while the parents deal with their difficulties, or to offer a permanent placement if the child is unable to return home.

An FGC cannot be carried out half-heartedly and must be convened independently of the child protection or care proceedings process.

It requires thorough preparation of the parents and other family members to ensure that all of the options available to the child are properly and fully considered. It may be necessary to hold more than one FGC, involving perhaps the maternal and paternal families separately. Even if a father is not involved in the child's life, his family should be invited to contribute to the conference to give the child the best chance of being brought up within their birth family, and to ensure that all possibilities of family care are explored before action is considered to allow placement of the child elsewhere.

It is not uncommon for parents to conceal from their family or minimise the seriousness of the concerns about the child until close to the end of care proceedings. It may be that they cannot accept the strength of the case for removal of their child until they have seen the final reports, and it may only be at that stage that they begin to involve their wider family and put forward suggestions for alternative carers. This can lead to considerable delay for the child while those carers are being assessed, which could have been avoided by a careful FGC before or at the beginning of proceedings.

Many local authorities have developed their own FGC teams, and the charity Family Rights Group is taking the lead on developing good practice for FGCs. They have published guidance on holding FGCs and can provide links to organisations able to provide local FGC conveners (Family Rights Group, 2012).

The No Order Principle

In England, Wales and Northern Ireland, the courts may not make an order in respect of a child unless the making of that order is better for the child than not making an order. This means that not only does the local authority taking care proceedings have to satisfy the court about the factual basis for their case, i.e. that the threshold criteria have been met, but also that an order is necessary.

You may be able to show that a child has suffered significant harm as a result of his parent's care, or lack of it, but if the parents are willing to place the child with a relative or friend who can protect the child adequately, or are willing to make the necessary changes to the child's circumstances, the court will not make a care order.

> *Where a court is considering whether or not to make one or more orders under this Act with respect to a child, it shall not make the order or any of the orders unless it considers that doing so would be better for the child than making no order at all.*
>
> *Children Act 1989 s.1(5) and Children (Northern Ireland) Order 1985 s.3(5)*

Avoiding delay

In coming to a decision about a child's future, the court must bear in mind that, in general, any delay in making that decision will not be in the child's best interests. The local authority should act on the same principle, and should not delay in starting the court process if it seems likely that intervention is going to be required. Even with the requirement of the Children and Families Act 2014 amendment to s32(i)(a) of the Children Act 1989 that care proceedings must be concluded within 26 weeks, a child can spend a significant amount of time without knowing where he will be spending the rest of his childhood. That time should not be extended by delays in beginning proceedings if they are necessary.

> *In any proceedings in which any question with respect to the upbringing of a child arises, the court shall have regard to the general principle that any delay in determining the question is likely to prejudice the welfare of the child.*
>
> *Children Act 1989 s.1(2) and Children (Northern Ireland) Order 1985 s.3(2)*

TIP 2

Get the paperwork right

The importance of getting the paperwork right cannot be underestimated. If there are errors in this, it can result in significant delays for the child.

Getting authority to start proceedings

Legal proceedings are issued in the name of the local authority. In each local authority there will be an officer authorised to start proceedings, usually the Director of Children's Services. That authority will usually be delegated to a Head of Social Care or other senior manager and you will need to check your own organisation's policies and procedures on who needs to authorise making an application.

In many local authorities you may have to make the case for proceedings to a senior manager or internal panel, if there is time. You will need to take legal advice on whether your case is strong enough to justify proceedings and how to establish the legal framework for the outcome you want to achieve.

Pre-proceedings checklist

In England and Wales, the *Public Law Outline* (guidance issued by the Ministry of Justice) provides a pre-proceedings checklist to promote good case preparation (Ministry of Justice, 2014a). It sets out the documents that the court will expect to see filed with the application and disclosed to the other parties in the proceedings. It is accepted that in some cases urgent action will be required to protect a child and there will not be time to prepare all the required documents, but the basic principle is that all parties, including the court, should have as much relevant information about the child and family as possible, as soon as possible, so that timely and well-informed decisions can be made about the child.

Pre-proceedings checklist
The checklist documents

- Previous court orders and judgments/reasons

- Any relevant assessment materials
  - Initial and core assessments
  - Section 7 and 37 reports
  - Relatives and friends materials (e.g. a genogram)

- Other relevant reports and records
  - Single, joint or inter-agency materials (e.g. health and education/Home Office and immigration documents)
  - Records of discussions with the family
  - Key local authority minutes and records for the child (including Strategy Discussion Record)

- Pre-existing care plans (e.g. child in need plan, looked after child plan and child protection plan)

- Social work chronology

- Letters before proceedings

Documents to be prepared for the proceedings

- Schedule of Proposed Findings

- Initial Social Work Statement

- Care Plan

- Allocation Record and Timetable for the Child

Ministry of Justice (2014b)

Application forms

All courts have standard application forms that must be completed in order to start proceedings. Careful completion of these forms is essential, as errors or omissions could prove fatal to the application, or cause delay in the progress of the case. Check your organisation's procedure manual to establish who has responsibility for completing the forms. Do you submit a draft to the legal department for checking and issue, or does the legal department draft the forms and send them to you to authorise? Either way, you must ensure that the details on the form are correct and up to date.

Blank copies of the forms that are used to apply for different orders are available from the Ministry of Justice website at www.justice.gov.uk/courts/procedure-rules/family/formspage. These can be useful to understand what is needed for each application, although most legal departments will have electronic copies on their own systems that will be used for the filed version.

Once the court has issued the forms, they will be sent out to the parties at the addresses that you have provided. If the child's parents do not receive the application, they will not be able to be involved in the proceedings and they will have been deprived of their right to a fair trial. Even final court decisions can be set aside if a parent has not been given notice of the proceedings.

Consider the following points.

- Is the address you have on file the most recent for each parent?

- Is there a father with parental responsibility who isn't around? Even if he has had no contact with the child for years, he will automatically be a party to the proceedings. He will have the right to be informed about and involved in all matters concerning his child. A father without parental responsibility will not automatically be a party to the proceedings, but should be given notice that an application is being made and have the opportunity to apply to be joined to the case.

- Is the child being looked after by a friend or relative? They need to be informed of the proceedings.

- Has the mother moved to a refuge, or is there another reason why the address of a party or the child should be kept secret? If so, make sure that your lawyer knows to leave the address off the forms and to make the necessary application to the court to withhold the address.

- Have there been problems with correspondence to a home address in the past? The court can make a direction for the paperwork to be sent to an alternative address where the party is more likely to receive it.

- Is there an international element to the case? If a parent or child is usually resident in another country, or there have been proceedings in another country, the 1996 Hague Convention on Jurisdiction, Applicable Law, Recognition, Enforcement and Co-operation in Respect of Parental Responsibility and Measures for the Protection of Children of Brussels II Revised may apply. Both of these kinds of cases require co-operation between countries concerned with a child and may involve the case being transferred to another state. Legal advice should be taken about whether another country should be informed. The International Child Abduction and Contact Unit acts as a point of contact between the UK and other states and can advise on cases with an international element (Ministry of Justice, 2013).

Where it is safe to do so, it is good practice for the social worker who has a relationship with the family to take the application forms to the parents, to explain what they mean and to encourage them to seek independent legal advice. This will be particularly important where parents have mental health or learning difficulties, and other professionals may need to be involved to support them.

If a parent has mental health or learning difficulties, the court will need to know if there are concerns that they might not have the capacity to follow the court proceedings or to give instructions to their lawyers. Sometimes it will be sufficient to have an independent advocate with them to provide support and ensure that they are following proceedings, but where there are serious doubts about the capacity of an adult in proceedings, the court may invite the Official Solicitor to represent that person.

The Official Solicitor is an arm's length department of the Ministry of Justice and acts as a litigation friend for vulnerable adults. It is a publicly funded service with considerable pressure on its resources and can be a significant source of delay in children's cases. Before they can agree to act, they will need to see medical evidence that the child's parent lacks the capacity to conduct proceedings and that there is no other person who is able to act for them.

It will help reduce delay if you can flag up with your legal department, and through them the court, the likelihood that the Official Solicitor may be needed and provide any medical reports you have that would indicate the need for the Official Solicitor's appointment.

Have a good chronology, but don't overload it

One of the most important documents in the case will be the social work chronology. It should set out a complete history of the child and previous history of the family, if relevant. A good chronology can create a clear factual picture of the family and present a lot of information in a concise and easy-to-follow format.

In an ideal world, a child's social work file will have a good chronology on it already which can be filed with the court with little or no editing. In reality, these chronologies may often need summarising and condensing to avoid overwhelming the court with reams of paper and repeated entries. For example, if the state of the house is an issue and you have made five home visits and noted no improvement, group these visits together in one time period rather than list each date and repeat 'no change' as an entry.

Administrative events need not be included – the court doesn't need to know that you had to make five phone calls and send two emails to a support service before they accepted a referral.

Ideally, each entry in a chronology should be kept to one or two lines. Bear in mind that details of the most relevant information will be set out in full elsewhere in the paperwork – the chronology simply puts it in context and on a timeline.

An entry that says 'Child attended school with bruises on face, no adequate explanation given' followed by an entry reading 'Medical examination by Dr A, conclusion possible non-accidental injury' gives all the necessary information and a reader will find Dr A's report filed elsewhere in the paperwork, with all the details of what has been said in explanation and exactly where the bruises were. This entry does not require a paragraph of explanation about how the school made a referral, or about the arrangements that you made to set up the medical.

Information has more impact in brief, relevant bullet points. Three reported incidents of violence on the same page of a chronology create a more powerful impression of the sustained harm experienced by the child than one incident on each of three separate pages with paragraphs of description spacing them out, even though the timeline will be the same.

Writing a statement

A statement should not repeat the chronology, nor should it repeat detailed information contained in reports or assessments that will be available to the court. It should be as brief as possible, sticking strictly to relevant matters. The basic history of the child is set out in the chronology, and the incidents in the past have not been enough to trigger care proceedings before. You need to explain what has happened to the child recently and why this means that court intervention is needed now. Particularly where the application is to change a child's placement at the start of proceedings, it is important to explain what harm you think that the child is likely to suffer if an order is not made. You must also consider the pros and cons of each possible outcome of the hearing to show why you are asking for a particular order, rather than just arguing for the order that you want.

The court should rely on the social worker as an expert to provide analysis of the situation facing the child, so you should not restrict yourself to the bare facts, but explain what you think are the relevant issues in the case and how you think that they should be resolved to the benefit of the child.

The Public Law Outline (Ministry of Justice, 2014b) sets out what is required in an initial social work statement in England and Wales.

INITIAL SOCIAL WORK STATEMENT

This means a statement prepared by the local authority strictly limited to the following evidence:

(a) the precipitating incident(s) and background circumstances relevant to the grounds and reasons for making the application including a brief description of any referral and assessment processes that have already occurred;

(b) any facts and matters that are within the social worker's personal knowledge limited to the findings sought by the local authority;

(c) any emergency steps and previous court orders that are relevant to the application;

(d) any decisions made by the local authority that are relevant to the application;

(e) information relevant to the ethnicity, language, religion, culture, gender and vulnerability of the child and other significant persons in the form of a 'family profile' together with a narrative description and details of the social care and other services that are relevant to the same;

(f) where the local authority is applying for an interim order: the local authority's initial proposals for the child (which are also to be set out in the Care Plan) including placement, contact with parents and other significant persons and the social care services that are proposed;

(g) the local authority's initial proposals for the further assessment of the parties during the proceedings including twin track/concurrent planning (where more than one permanence option for the child is being explored by the local authority)

The Department for Education has issued Statutory Guidance on court orders and pre-proceedings which sets out the requirements for statements and includes an evidence template (2014). Most local authorities will have a standard form of witness statement on their electronic systems to be completed, and BAAF publishes a pro-forma combined Child Placement Report and Annex B report which can be used to support applications for placement orders.

The most important part of the social work statement is the analysis. Unless you are dealing with an unexplained injury with possible complex medical conditions, the facts are usually either agreed or fairly easy to establish. The major area of difference between children's services and the child's parents is usually what the facts mean for the care of the child in the future. The courts have complained frequently about the lack of analysis in social work statements, as they are relying on social workers' expertise to inform their decisions, not just looking for reports of facts.

In some respects the reports of the guardian and the social worker, and the social worker's statement, are very detailed, giving information about health and likes and dislikes, wishes and feelings. However, there is surprisingly little detail about the central issue of the type of placement that will best meet the children's needs...In part, this may be an unfortunate by-product of the entirely proper use,

> *by both witnesses, of the checklist of factors and, in*
> *the case of the social worker's placement report, of*
> *the required pro forma. However, the court requires*
> *not only a list of the factors that are relevant to the*
> *central decision but also a narrative account of how*
> *they fit together, including an analysis of the pros*
> *and cons of the various orders that might*
> *realistically be under consideration given the*
> *circumstances of the children, and a fully reasoned*
> *recommendation.*
>
> *Plymouth CC v G (children) [2010] EWCA Civ 1271*

In 2013, the President of the Family Division (quoted below) noted that matters had not improved and gave some strongly worded opinions about the standard of reasoning and analysis of social workers, Guardians and judges. He was dealing particularly with cases where the plan for the child was adoption, and emphasised that all of the pros and cons of all of the options must be properly considered before an order can be made. If the analysis is lacking, the application must be adjourned to allow further evidence and statements to be filed to give the court the information it requires before making an order, even if that means the proceedings will stretch out longer than 26 weeks.

> *We have real concerns, shared by other judges,*
> *about the recurrent inadequacy of the analysis and*
> *reasoning put forward in support of the case for*
> *adoption, both in the materials put before the court*
> *by local authorities and guardians and also in too*
> *many judgments. This is nothing new. But it is time*
> *to call a halt.*
>
> *Most experienced family judges will unhappily have*

> *had too much exposure to material as anodyne and inadequate as that described here by Ryder LJ. This sloppy practice must stop. It is simply unacceptable in a forensic context where the issues are so grave and the stakes, for both child and parent, so high.*
>
> *We emphasise the words 'global, holistic evaluation'. This point is crucial. The judicial task is to evaluate all the options, undertaking a global, holistic and multi-faceted evaluation of the child's welfare which takes into account all the negatives and the positives, all the pros and cons, of each option.*
>
> Re B-S (Children) [2013] EWCA Civ 1146

Although the President was dealing with an adoption case, the principle has been extended to fostering cases, and the approach is needed wherever separation of parent and child is being considered. Rather than an analysis moving along a line of severity, dismissing each option in turn, the statement must look at each option thoroughly, considering both the positives and negatives for the child of every potential order, before making a final recommendation in the best interests of the child.

In addition to the advantages and disadvantages of each option, the court must consider whether the local authority can provide support services that would allow a child to remain at home or in a family placement rather than being removed into care. The social work statement must include consideration of services that might be available to the family and, if appropriate, reasons why those services are not being provided. The court is directed to be alert to the possibility of resource issues guiding the local authority's thinking and to ask questions if they think that this is happening. The statement should include the reasons why any potentially appropriate services are being withheld, if that is the case.

Involvement in private proceedings

Care proceedings are not the only cases in which local authority social workers may be required to go to court. Where parents have made applications for child arrangement orders (previously residence, contact or specific issue orders), the court may request a social worker from the local authority to provide a statement, or even simply to attend court to give oral evidence, on an issue that is relevant to the case. The court may request evidence under s.7 of the Children Act 1989, usually when the local authority has had some relevant involvement with the family, and will specify the particular information that they require from the local authority.

The court can also request a local authority to conduct an investigation under s.37 of the Children Act 1989. This may happen when the evidence in a private case gives cause for concern; perhaps one parent will allege that the other is abusing or neglecting the child, or the court may think that the child is at risk of significant harm because of the volatility or intensity of the antagonism between her parents. If the court is really concerned, it may make an interim care or supervision order at the same time as ordering an investigation. If a s.37 investigation is ordered, the local authority must consider the child's circumstances and decide whether to offer services to the family or to apply for a care or supervision order to protect the child. The local authority must prepare a statement to the court explaining their reasons for the decisions they have made.

Where a court requests a s.7 or s.37 report, a standard form witness statement can be used and adapted to respond to the specific requirements of the order made.

Where an adoption application is made, the local authority has a duty to prepare a report for the court in respect of the application. This must be in the form of an Annex A report (named after Annex A of Practice Direction 14C of the Family Procedure Rules 2010). Where the child has been placed for adoption from care by a local authority, the information in the Annex A report will involve a significant level of duplication or updating of the Annex B report used when applying for a placement order. Most of the factual information required will be available on the child's and the adopter's files. Where the application is for a step-parent adoption, an intercountry adoption or adoption following on from any other private arrangement, there may have been no previous contact between the family and the local authority. The report and the information required is the same for a private adoption of this sort as it is for the adoption of children from care, and several visits to the family and further investigation will be required before the report can be completed.

In care proceedings, the witness statements are served on (meaning formally delivered to) all other parties in the case, unless the court has given specific directions to withhold something that needs to be kept confidential. In private proceedings, the local authority social worker is being asked to provide a report for the court, not to act as a witness for one side or the other. The report must be sent to the court only, and the judge will decide who will see any or all of the report. This is particularly important in adoption cases, where the birth parents may be parties, but may need to be prevented from having identifying information about the adopters. The same rule applies to reports on special guardianship order (SGO) applications. Even if the SGO application is made within care proceedings, the report prepared is a report for the court, not a witness statement to be distributed to all parties. The court will usually then disclose it to other parties, but this is a decision that must be left to the court.

Social workers may be called to give evidence in criminal proceedings, where they are involved in a case of child abuse, or where they witness an assault or other crime in the course of their work. There are strict rules of evidence in criminal cases, which do not apply in family cases; in particular, the witness can only report events that they have actually seen, not things that they have been told (rule against hearsay). If you are called to give evidence in a criminal case, the police will usually take your statement by speaking to you and writing down the admissible evidence. You will then be asked to check it for accuracy and sign it before it is sent to prosecutors.

TIP 3

Prepare yourself (and relevant others) well for court

Re-read the papers

You will have been sent statements and reports by your legal department as they come in, but it can be really helpful to re-read them in one go, as the court will be doing, a day or two before the hearing. Re-reading your own statement is also a useful exercise, remembering what you thought was relevant at the time, and checking whether there was anything that you left out as less important but that might need to be re-evaluated in the light of later events.

Look at statements and reports that refer to your statements. If they are disputing facts, is there anything else in the file that supports you? If there is criticism of the local authority's actions, consider why things were done in that way and how you will answer any questions raised about those actions.

Speak to your legal department

Although court orders will usually set out a timetable that ensures that everyone involved will have statements and reports in good time for a hearing, timetables can slip and it is not unusual for documents to be filed at the last moment, sometimes actually on the morning of a court hearing. Ask your legal department on the day before the hearing whether anything new has been filed and get a copy to read and consider before the hearing. Trying to absorb a lengthy report in a busy court corridor is never going to be ideal. Equally, you should make your legal department aware of any new developments in the case as they happen – not letting them know for the first time at court. This gives the other lawyers the chance to check their clients' version of events and go through any new statements or reports before getting to court.

Take a colleague with you

If possible, it is helpful to have another worker, preferably a manager, at court with you. This gives you moral support and shows the family that the case is being brought by the local authority as an organisation, rather than giving the impression that you personally are attacking the family.

Check the date, time and address where the hearing is taking place

You will have been sent a copy of the court order fixing a hearing, but these things can change. If one case runs over time, a judge may put a morning hearing into the afternoon, or list a short hearing before the start of the main court day. One court region may have several different court locations and you may not be in the same building, or even in the same town, as you were for the last hearing.

21

If evidence hasn't been filed on time, one party may have requested and been granted an adjournment of the hearing to another day. A phone call to double-check where you need to be and at what time can save a lot of trouble and stress the next morning. If things have changed significantly, you could make sure that the child's parents are aware of the change, especially if they are not represented.

If non-professional witnesses are being called, you will need to make sure in advance that they are aware of the need to attend, where they are going and that they will need to bring all their relevant notes, recordings, etc, with them. The legal department will have written to witnesses with the expected timetable and when they will be required at court, but non-professional witnesses may require reminders and reassurance. If a foster carer is being called, make sure that arrangements are made for their foster child/ren to be cared for while the carer is at court.

In those rare cases where a child is required to give evidence in court, you should check that appropriate protective arrangements are in place. The way in which the child is going to give evidence – directly, from behind a screen or by video link – will have been directed by the court in advance, but it does no harm to check that the direction has reached the court staff responsible for making the practical arrangements. You may also need to reserve a separate waiting area for the child, or use a separate entrance to the court to avoid the child having to walk past or meet his parents or other members of the family.

Dressing for court

Lawyers have a dress code for court, witnesses do not, but it is still important to dress appropriately for court. Turning up to a High Court hearing in jeans and a T-shirt is not going to endear you to the judge – you are asking the court to trust your judgement on issues that will affect a family for the rest of their lives, so you cannot look as though you are taking the proceedings lightly; but on the other hand, it isn't necessary to try to look like a lawyer.

Wear ordinary, sensible work clothes, and make sure that you are comfortable. The court isn't going to know that you are fidgeting with your clothes because your collar is too tight or because you have just decided that your skirt is too short. They may simply see a witness who doesn't appear confident or comfortable with the evidence that they are giving.

Take the case file

Have the case file with you at court. You may have put everything you think relevant into a statement, but other parties may want to focus on quite different matters. Parties may want details of meetings, to see documents and challenge dates, all of which will need access to the files. Bear in mind your organisation's data protection policies for taking files out of the office, and don't leave case files unattended at court – courts are not secure places! Some courts can be quite cramped for space and you may need to take care that one party cannot read confidential information about another over your shoulder.

Carry some cash, including small change

You may need to provide copies of documents from the case file, receive faxes or print out documents. The court offices are usually able to help, but will charge and some provide coin-operated copiers.

Don't rely on the court timetable

It is not easy for courts to set their timetables rigidly. It is impossible to be completely accurate about how long each witness will take and the judge will not want to break the evidence of a witness across court days. A court may want to give judgement on the same day, and you cannot be sure that you will be able to leave court within normal working hours.

TIP 4

Understand how a court works

Court structure

In Northern Ireland, and in England and Wales until April 2014, the usual entry point of a case into the legal system was at the **Family Proceedings Court (FPC)**. FPCs are the only courts that can hear applications for emergency protection orders. This court is made up of lay magistrates, or justices, who usually sit in groups of three, although sometimes two will hear a case in an emergency. They are trained to make decisions in family cases, but do not have any formal legal qualifications. Some FPCs also employ legally qualified and experienced District Judges, who are able to hear cases alone.

FPCs will usually only list cases where the final hearing is expected to take two or three days, although those with District Judges may accept longer cases. Lay magistrates are not usually asked to deal with cases that involve legal complexities or conflicts of expert evidence.

Cases can be transferred upwards to the **County Courts**, or the most complex cases, including those with an international element, will be referred to the **High Court**. In each of those courts, cases will be heard by a judge, legally qualified and with experience of child care cases. There are different grades of judge and judges are sometimes referred to as having their "ticket", which qualifies them to hear cases of different complexities.

The High Court has some specific powers, under what is known as the "inherent jurisdiction", powers that do not come from any statute. If the High Court takes a child into wardship, effectively assuming parental responsibility for itself, it can make all necessary decisions for a child. It is this power that is used when a decision has to be made, for example, to withhold lifesaving treatment for a terminally ill child or to allow sterilisation of a teenage girl with learning difficulties.

The High Court also has access to a team of Tipstaffs, who have wide-ranging power of search and entry and can be used to seek and find a child who has been removed from care or is otherwise missing and at risk. These powers are rarely used, but remain available for those extraordinary cases where they may be the only way to protect a child adequately.

From April 2014, the family court system in England and Wales has become a single **Family Court**. All applications, except for those exercising the inherent jurisdiction or with an international aspect, will be made to the local designated family centre, which will then allocate the case to the appropriate judge or magistrates. High Court judges may sit as judges in the Family Court, or they may still sit as judges of the High Court when the inherent jurisdiction is needed or international cases specifically need a High Court order.

Parents and others may apply to the High Court for a judicial review of a local authority's decisions or actions. They can ask the court to rule on whether the local authority has acted fairly and reasonably. This power can be used outside care proceedings and has been used to challenge decisions not to provide services or not to accommodate a child in need.

Appeals can be made from magistrates and district judges to higher level judges and from those judges to the **Court of Appeal**. All except appeals from magistrates will need to obtain permission before being able to appeal. From the Court of Appeal, a case that raises a significant point of law can be appealed to the **Supreme Court** (formerly the House of Lords) and those that raise human rights issues may be the subject of application to the **European Court of Human Rights**.

Who's who in court

Courts may not always appear user-friendly, and it is often assumed that people know where to go and what to do. Security staff at the entrance to most court buildings will be able to tell you where to go to get information and where to find your court. Court Lists (the cases to be heard that day) are usually displayed near the entrance to the court, but in family cases, where the family's privacy is protected, they will often be listed by case number only, or by case number and local authority. The case number will be that allocated by the court, not the internal local authority reference, and can be found on notices, orders and correspondence from the court.

The first person you will usually meet at court is an usher or list caller. These are members of the court administrative staff who often wear short black robes as well as name badges to identify themselves. There may be one usher for each court, or one usher may cover several courts. It is important to report your arrival to them, as they will know whether other members of your team have arrived. Courts often have meeting rooms dotted around the building and it can be all too easy to miss each other.

Ushers will be going in and out of courtrooms taking witnesses into court, moving cases around or reporting to other court staff when cases are ready to be heard. In a family court building, do not follow an usher into court to announce your arrival; family proceedings are held in private and if a court is sitting you will be interrupting the proceedings just by walking in. You will need to wait outside.

If you are at court to give evidence in an adoption application, there may well need to be security arrangements in place to prevent the birth parents from identifying or coming into contact with the adopters. If the application is contested, the court will usually make arrangements for the parents and adopters to attend court on different days, but if it is possible that they will be in the building at the same time, the court should have made arrangements for them to be kept apart. If this is necessary, speak to your legal department to ensure that the court has been made aware of the position, and check where the adopters and birth parents will be waiting at court. Take care that the birth parents do not see you interacting with the adopters outside the building or in public areas of the court.

Figure 1: Who sits where in court

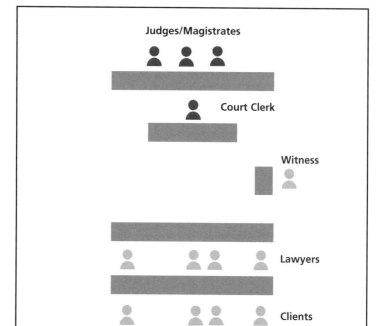

Inside the courtroom there will be a Bench where the judges or magistrates sit. In older courts this may be raised above the courtroom. In front of the Bench will be a desk for the court clerk or associate, an administrator, or, where the Bench is composed of lay magistrates, a qualified lawyer who provides legal advice to the magistrates.

Close to the front of the courtroom will be a witness box, which may be an enclosed box or, in more modern courtrooms, simply a desk and chair. Facing the Bench will be rows of desks or tables for lawyers and their clients.

In the most serious cases, leading counsel (senior lawyers, also known as silks or QCs) will sit in the front row. Other advocates will sit in the second row and solicitors, usually sitting with their clients, will sit behind them. The party applying for the order will sit at one end, the respondents in the middle and the child's representative at the other end.

If you are the caseworker, you will be expected to sit in court behind your lawyer throughout the proceedings. If you are attending court to give evidence on a specific aspect of the case, you may be asked to wait outside until the court is ready to hear from you. This will be to prevent your evidence from being contaminated or influenced by you having listened to other witnesses.

Forms of address

When you give evidence, you will be asked questions by the lawyers sitting in the well of the court, but you will be asked to address your answers to the Bench. The judge may also ask you questions directly. There are different forms of address for judges that depend both on their own rank and sometimes on the court in which they are sitting. A Circuit Judge will be addressed as 'Your Honour' in the County Court, but may sit on a case as a Judge of the High Court, in which case they will be addressed as 'My Lord'.

Getting a title wrong can show carelessness or inexperience, and can irritate a judge. You may occasionally hear a judge correcting a lawyer who has addressed the court wrongly, more usually if the lawyer has inadvertently "promoted" the judge, but they are less likely to correct a witness.

Judge sitting as:	Address as:
UK – Supreme Court, Court of Appeal; High Court Judge	My Lord/My Lady
County Court Circuit Judge or Recorder	Your Honour
High Court or County Court District Judge	Sir/Madam
District Judge and lay magistrates	Your Worship (slightly old-fashioned in England and Wales) or Sir/Madam

Your lawyer will know which title is appropriate for the judge sitting on the day, and you can ask them how to address the Bench, or simply follow what the lawyers are saying. If you're not sure about what to call the judge, the safest thing to do is call him/her Sir or Madam, which shows respect to the court and is unlikely to cause offence. If there is more than one person on the Bench, the one sitting in the middle will be the Chair, and remarks should be addressed to that person.

What to expect at court

There is a difference between what happens *in* court and what happens *at* court. Inside the courtroom is a formal process which, by and large, follows a set format to ensure that each party has a chance to put their case and gives the judge the information required to come to a decision. A lot of negotiation takes place at court, but outside the courtroom. Much of this will be administrative, timetabling and preparing draft orders and the way in which it will be done depends on the stage of the proceedings and to some extent on how acrimonious the hearing that day is likely to be. Sometimes all the lawyers, the Children's Guardian and the social worker will sit together and discuss proposals for the way forward, but sometimes each party to a case will be in their own separate room, with lawyers shuttling backwards and forwards taking instructions and passing on suggestions.

You should not get involved in discussions with other parties' lawyers without your own lawyer being present. It is a breach of the lawyer's code of conduct to communicate directly with another party when that party is also represented by a lawyer, but this is sometimes forgotten when the party is a local authority and you are there as a fellow professional.

You should also remember that lawyers, particularly barristers, have to be professional chameleons. An advocate could be representing your local authority, backing children's services to the hilt, for nine cases in a row, but act for a parent on the tenth, forcefully attacking the social workers and their decisions. You may have a close working relationship with a lawyer, but if they are at court representing another party you should be careful to limit your interaction with them to social pleasantries. Find the local authority's lawyer for that day and establish how things are going to run before getting involved in any discussions about the case.

Often negotiations outside court can result in an agreed order, which will then be taken into court for approval by the judge. If there are sticking points on the progress of the case, the court can often make a ruling on submissions from lawyers only, and it is only usually where there are serious disputes about the facts or the care plan that a social worker would be required to give evidence at hearings other than the final hearing.

TIP 5

Consider all the options for the child

You may be focused on one particular outcome of your case, which you or your organisation have decided is in the best interests of the child concerned, but family courts have a wide discretion to do what they think is best, and it is not simply a matter of granting or refusing your application for a particular order.

The court can make a wide range of orders – not just the order you have requested

The court cannot make an order for the adoption of a child unless there has been a specific application for an adoption order. However, in all family proceedings cases, including adoption applications, the court can make any other order it considers appropriate. In one extreme case in which prospective adopters of a child from an African country applied for an adoption order, the court decided that there were concerns about child trafficking and exploitation and the child was instead placed in the care of the local authority under an interim care order.

Think about other possible orders

Consider how the child will best be protected if the court refuses to make the order for which you have asked. Talk through the options with your lawyer so that they are ready to jump up with suggestions if things go against you. If you are asking for an interim care order and the court orders placement with a relative under a child arrangements order, consider whether this should be combined with a supervision order, or an order limiting contact with the parents. Would a family assessment order allow the local authority some of the access to the child that you have been refused by the birth parents? These questions need to be considered in advance, as there will be a very small window of opportunity to ask the court to add to the order that they are considering, and if you come up with a useful alternative on the way out of the court door it will be too late.

Have your arguments ready for why other options are not appropriate

Courts will often give an indication of the way that they are thinking, and rather than springing a surprise decision at the end of a hearing, will give the affected party an opportunity to give their opinion. They may do this either by asking their own questions during evidence, or by making a suggestion and allowing your lawyer to make submissions. If you have anticipated the possibility and have a coherent answer to the judge's question, 'Why should I not order….?' you stand a much better chance of being taken seriously than if you "um" and "er" while trying to think of a good reason.

If the court doesn't make the order you recommend, what other ways could there be to protect the child?

If your application is refused, it might not be because the court thinks that the child is safe in their parents' care; it may simply be that you haven't been able to provide enough evidence to justify the making of an order. If you believe that the child is still at risk, you will need to have a child protection plan in place. Be aware that you could find it becomes more difficult to work with a family after a court case, as they may see the court's decision as declaring them "innocent" or as not accepting any of your concerns.

TIP 6

Understand what your lawyer can or cannot do

Lawyers were traditionally viewed as rather a breed apart. They used a different language with words from ancient French and Latin, and wore peculiar costumes, sometimes including wigs. Lawyers have changed, and the system has modernised. Robes are no longer worn in family courts and Latin phrases are no longer part of the court's vocabulary. The lawyers, and the courts, are part of the child protection system, and their place in that system needs to be understood to enable them to be used effectively.

Understand the lawyer's role

The role of the lawyer is to present their client's case to the best of their ability. They do not have to agree with their client and cannot compel their client to follow their advice. They have a duty to the court not to mislead the court, and in family cases lawyers are encouraged to act collaboratively in the interests of the child.

In child care cases the local authority is the client; as a social worker, you are at court representing the local authority and therefore you are the client.

Giving instructions/taking advice

As the client, you give the lawyer instructions which, unless they involve dishonesty or misleading the court, they must follow. Lawyers can and should advise their clients on the likely outcome of the case, the likely consequences of any course of action they intend to pursue, and the best way of using the law and the court to achieve their desired outcome. There is no duty on the social worker as a client to follow the advice given them by their lawyer. There will be some cases where the welfare of the child is incompatible with legal advice. In those cases, the lawyer's duty is to set out the legal position and warn the client of any consequences of failing to follow their advice.

For a local authority, decisions could be open to challenge by way of judicial review, and a local authority pursuing a course in court against legal advice will need to be able to show that their decision was both lawful and reasonable.

The final decision on how to run a case rests with the client department, i.e. with the social worker, as the department's representative on the ground at court, deciding whether or not to follow legal advice and what instructions to give the lawyer. If you decide to follow a course against legal advice, you could be exposing the local authority to criticism, further legal actions or costs, and you should obtain clear authority from an appropriate manager for taking such a course.

Discussions outside court

Much of the detail of the progress of a case can be agreed between the parties either before they go into court or after the judge has given an indication of the way they want a case to go. A parent may be willing to agree that their child should be placed in foster care, but not accept your care plan for contact, or put forward a plan for the child to be cared for by a relative. This may give scope for agreement to be reached outside court.

Be aware of the limitations of your authority to agree use of resources; you may be able to agree to the provision of a bus pass to help the parents to attend contact, but have to get a manager's authority before you can agree to fund taxis. You can put the local authority in a very awkward position if you let the case go forward with an agreement that the local authority will act in a certain way if you are then refused the resources to carry out that action.

You can be put under some pressure to agree something on the spot by other parties outside court, and sometimes by your own lawyer if they do not understand the internal requirements of your department. You need to explain that you are not being awkward, but that there are some things that you do not have the power to agree. If you make the position clear to your lawyer, they will be able to support you in resisting pressure from the other parties and allow you to follow your department's policies and procedures wherever necessary.

What the lawyer cannot do

Your lawyer, even if directly employed by the local authority, cannot make decisions on behalf of the local authority. Sometimes the lawyer will have been involved with a case for longer than the social work team, especially if the structure of children's services means that the case is transferred from a duty team to a children in need team, then to a looked after children team as it progresses through the system. They may therefore have more direct experience of the case than you or other social workers.

It can sometimes be tempting, both for the lawyer and for you as the social worker, to regard the lawyer as having some insight into the case. However, they do not have any social work expertise and have no responsibility for making any decisions about their cases. If you are asked to make a decision at court that you are not sure about, contact a social work manager rather than expecting or allowing your lawyer to make that decision for you.

Lawyers can support your court attendance; they can give you an idea of what to expect and participate in general training around court skills. What they cannot do is rehearse your evidence in a particular case. The barristers' Code of Conduct says that 'a barrister must not rehearse, practise or coach a witness in relation to his/her evidence' (Bar Standards Board, 2014, Rule 11.4). There is a fine line to be drawn between giving a witness an idea of what to expect – 'We'll need to go into detail about the events of that weekend, so make sure that you're clear about everything that happened' – which is acceptable, and coaching – 'When I ask you about that visit, make sure that you tell me that she was threatening towards you' – which is unethical.

If a lawyer gives court skills training with a mock trial, they must not use a scenario that is similar to a case that they will be conducting with you. You cannot expect a lawyer to tell you what questions they are going to ask you, or tell you what you should answer to questions from the other lawyers in the case. If they refuse to do so, they are not being unhelpful – they are following their own code of professional ethics.

Once you are in the witness box, you are pretty much on your own. In films and television dramas, lawyers are often seen jumping up to intervene with 'Objection!' or complaints that another lawyer is "badgering the witness". In reality, most lawyers will treat you as a witness with respect, and will work to their own professional standards. You are a professional witness and are expected to be able to take a certain amount of challenge. You should not expect your lawyer to protect you from robust questioning and it might seem undermining of your professional abilities if they were to do so.

TIP 7

Work with the Children's Guardian

A Children's Guardian (in England and Wales, Guardian ad Litem in Northern Ireland) is appointed in care and related proceedings to represent the child's interests and to assist the court in reaching a decision in the best interests of the child. They are independent from the local authority and work with an independent solicitor representing the child.

Understand the Guardian's role and duties

The responsibility of the Children's Guardian is to safeguard and promote the welfare of individual children who are the subject of family court proceedings by providing independent social work advice to the court. Guardians are social workers who have at least three years of post-qualification experience. They are expected to meet the child and be able to establish and represent the child's wishes and feelings to the court. They scrutinise the local authority's evidence and care plan and make their own recommendations to the court as to whether it is appropriate or not.

If the Guardian is representing an older child whose views conflict with those of the Guardian, the child may be separately represented in court by their solicitor and the Guardian will present their own views, sometimes without legal representation.

The Guardian has the right to see all local authority records relating to the child. In the past the Guardian would attend social services offices at the beginning of proceedings and read the entire file. Pressure on budgets and the increasing workload of Guardians means that this is not now always the case and they may just ask to see the documents or reports that they consider the most relevant.

In the past, Guardians were highly experienced social workers who had had significant experience, usually of managing a social work team within a local authority. They were mostly self-employed and able to manage their own time, which meant that they were able to spend time with a child and establish a real relationship with them. Their views were highly respected by the court, as they were able to focus on the situation of the specific child without the other pressures that a local authority social worker has to deal with. Like every other publicly funded service, the Guardians service has been subject to financial restraints and has lost many of the self-employed Guardians.

A social worker may become a Guardian now with only three years of post-qualification experience. Workloads are high and although they are still expected to meet the child, they are not required to see him more than two or three times during care proceedings. However, in many courts Guardians are still more respected than social workers and some courts may be more likely to accept their analysis of a case. In any event, it is likely be much easier to run a case when the Guardian shares the local authority's views than when there is conflict. Establishing a positive working relationship with the Guardian when he or she is appointed can only help proceedings. Bear in mind also that Guardians are usually appointed from a local office, so your relationship with the Guardian on your first case together may well have an impact on later proceedings.

In some cases, the child will be required to come to court to give evidence. The court will usually try and avoid this for young children especially, but older children may insist on coming to court either to hear the case or to put their own point of view. This will be an issue for the court to decide, but it is becoming more common as courts and lawyers are gaining more skill in dealing with child witnesses, and there is increasing emphasis on the right of the child to be directly involved in proceedings concerning their future.

It is possible to arrange familiarisation visits for children to come to court, see the courtroom and be helped to understand the legal process. Sometimes it will be appropriate for a child to meet the judge privately – not to give evidence, but so that the child can see who will be making decisions about his future. Judges have clear guidelines for this (Judiciary of England and Wales, 2010). Depending on the circumstances, it may be more appropriate for the social worker or for the Children's Guardian to take the lead in making arrangements and in accompanying the child to court. The child might also be more comfortable if their foster carer comes to court with them.

These arrangements should be discussed well in advance and each person's role clearly agreed, so that the child has a sense of a team of adults working together to support them through a potentially difficult process.

Keep the Guardian informed of any changes

A Guardian is more likely to support a local authority's actions if they are kept informed of the reasons behind each decision. They should be kept informed of significant events and local authority decisions relating to the child as they happen rather than discovering what has happened at the next hearing, when a statement is filed or when they are contacted by the parents complaining about a decision made by the local authority.

Invite the Guardian to the right meetings

Working Together to Safeguard Children (Statutory Guidance in England) says that a Children's Guardian 'should be invited to all formal planning meetings convened by the local authority in respect of the child. This includes statutory reviews of children who are accommodated or looked after, child protection conferences and relevant adoption panel meetings' (Department for Education, 2013). Guardians may not have the time to attend all, or indeed any, of these meetings, but the fact that they are invited allows them to consider any reports prepared for the meetings and to submit their opinions if they wish.

Be aware of the boundaries of the Guardian's role

The Children's Guardian can scrutinise the local authority's plans and actions and can attend meetings and give her opinions on the plans for the child. She is not part of the decision making process and does not have a vote on panels. The Guardian has no power to compel a local authority to follow her wishes, but can make applications to the court on the child's behalf if she feels that the local authority has acted unreasonably. A common area of conflict with Guardians is the choice of placement for a child, often because the Guardian is concerned with one particular child only, whereas the local authority has to balance the resources available to one child against the needs of all the other children for whom it is responsible.

CASE STUDY

A young child was accommodated in a specialist foster placement in order to carry out an assessment of her mother's ability to care for her. After some months, the assessment came to an end and the local authority's plan was to move the child to a mainstream foster placement during care proceedings. The Children's Guardian opposed the move, believing that it was in the child's best interests to minimise the number of placement moves. The social worker accepted that position, but her managers refused to continue funding the specialist placement for a child who no longer needed the particular skills of that foster carer.

The Guardian asked the court to compel the local authority to leave the child in placement. The Court of

Appeal refused to make any order, reinforcing previous case law that the choice of placement for a child under an interim care order is for the local authority alone, and neither the court nor the Children's Guardian can interfere with that choice.

Re M (A Child) [2009] EWCA Civ 1486

Listen to the Guardian's opinion – but form your own

Many Guardians have considerable experience of social work and of court proceedings. They are also able to bring a fresh and independent perspective to the situation. Their opinions should be listened to, particularly as you will have to address any differences in court. If you can resolve any differences before you get into court, having the Guardian's support will make court hearings easier. However, Guardians are not infallible and they should not be allowed to take over management of the case.

As a social worker, you have an individual professional responsibility to your client, the child in the case. Other professionals may have a different view as to the best interests of the child, but you need to have sufficient confidence in your own professional expertise to be able to consider others' points of view and make your own decisions on which views you should accept or reject. The Children's Guardian is simply one of a number of professionals who will have an opinion about the case and you have no obligation to accept or prefer one opinion over another.

A potentially difficult situation is where you hold one view on a case, but your managers hold a different view. Often this can be where you think that a particular service or resource will benefit the child for whom you are responsible, but they refuse access to it, either because the circumstances fail to meet their criteria, or because there are other cases with a higher need for that particular resource. These sorts of disagreements are not fatal to a local authority's case and there is no need to try to gloss over such differences or to compromise your professional opinions.

If you are asked about differences of approach, your responsibility is to give your opinion based on your professional training and experience. If other parties want to challenge the local authority's decision, they will need to call the managers responsible for making that decision. If this situation is likely to arise, it is a good idea to discuss it with your managers beforehand. You need to ensure that your managers understand your views and that they can explain to you why they do not share them.

If you can accept their position without sharing it, you will be able to explain the local authority's case to the court, for example, where you think that a family would probably benefit from a service but managers have decided that the cost benefit analysis prefers the allocation of that resource to another family. If the disagreement is more fundamental, for example, if you believe that the child is not at risk of significant harm when your managers believe otherwise, you need to give your managers enough notice of your position to enable them to produce the evidence that they will need to prove their case, rather than relying on your statement alone.

TIP 8

Learn how to perform well in court

The first thing to do when going into court is to turn your mobile phone off. The second thing to do is to check that your mobile phone is turned off. Very little irritates a judge more than a phone ringing in court.

Where to sit

If you are the case worker, you will sit in court behind your lawyer throughout the case. If you are simply attending court to give evidence, you will usually be expected to wait outside the courtroom until you are needed. Sometimes it might be helpful for you to hear evidence being given by another witness before giving your own, and if that is the case your lawyer can ask the court for permission for you to come into court to listen to the proceedings.

When it is time for you to give evidence, the court usher will show you where to go.

Giving evidence, taking an oath/affirmation, stand or sit

When giving evidence you will be referred to as being "in the witness box". In older court buildings or higher courts, this will be a partially enclosed space at the front of the courtroom; in newer courts and Family Proceedings Courts this is more likely to be a table or desk near the front. It will usually be to one side of the room to enable everybody to see the witness, and will be close to the judge or magistrates hearing the case.

You will be asked to take an oath to tell the truth, the whole truth and nothing but the truth. The usher will usually ask you if you are willing to be sworn on the Bible. Courts will have copies of the religious texts of the most common religions and you can ask to be sworn on whichever of those is appropriate for your faith. The oath begins 'I swear by Almighty God...' but is adapted to suit the appropriate religion.

If you are not religious, or your faith does not allow you to take an oath, you may ask to affirm. The form of words used in an affirmation is 'I do solemnly, sincerely and truly declare and affirm that the evidence I shall give shall be the truth, the whole truth and nothing but the truth'. You may also want to affirm rather than take an oath if your faith requires some ritual before an oath can be taken.

If you want to take an oath and need to carry out some action as part of the exercise, for example, a ritual handwashing, the courts will do their best to make reasonable provision for you to do so. It will be helpful if you can let the usher know in advance what you want to do so that they can have the appropriate book and oath card ready and make any other provision that you require.

The court will not investigate why you choose one form of oath or affirmation; the important thing is that you understand that you have an obligation to tell the truth. Whatever form of oath or affirmation you choose, the legal obligation to tell the truth will be the same, and you could face criminal prosecution if you give false evidence.

The usher will give you the appropriate book, if any, and a card with the right form of words. The book may be handed over in a cloth bag if there are religious restrictions on touching it; it will be for you to take it out if your faith requires it. You take the oath standing, holding the book in one hand and reading the words on the oath card. You will then usually be invited to sit while giving evidence. Some people prefer to stand, to put themselves on an equal level with the lawyers who usually (but not always) stand to speak. If you are not asked to sit and you are uncomfortable standing for any length of time, say that you would rather sit down.

The first questions will be asked by your lawyer. You will be asked to confirm your identity, name, job title and employer, and possibly your professional address. You will then be shown a copy of the statement you have made, usually by referring to a page number in the court bundle. You will be expected to look at it and confirm that it is your statement. You will probably be asked whether you want to change or add anything to that statement.

The lawyer who has called you (the local authority lawyer if you are a children's services social worker) will ask questions first, followed by the parents' lawyers and then the child's lawyer. The first lawyer then has an opportunity to ask any questions to clear up matters that have come up in the course of the other parties' questions. This is known as *Examination in Chief*, then *Cross-Examination* and finally *Re-examination*. The judge may interrupt you or the lawyers and ask questions at any time to clarify a point, or may wait until the end of the evidence and ask questions then.

Address your answers to the Bench

You will be asked questions by the lawyers, but it is important that your answers are heard by everyone, particularly the judge or magistrates. You will need to speak quite loudly; if there are microphones in front of you they will be for recording the evidence, not for amplifying your voice. You may be asked to 'address your answers to the Bench'. The easiest way to remember to do this is to angle your chair, or to stand, so that you are facing the judge. You will then have to turn your head to look at the lawyer asking the questions, but your answers will be directed to the judge.

Even if the evidence is being recorded, transcripts will only be prepared if there is an appeal. In making their decisions, judges will rely on the notes that they take at the time. To make sure that what you say is noted, give clear, short answers and watch the judge's pen (or keyboard). Give your answer in short sections and wait for the judge to finish writing it down before going on to the next section.

If the question is too complicated, ask for it to be broken down

Sometimes, particularly during cross-examination, the lawyer will try suggesting different situations or theories to you. This can be confusing and can result in misunderstandings about which part of the question you are answering. If you're not completely clear about what is being asked, it is perfectly reasonable to ask the lawyer to explain her question or to break it down into parts to ensure that everybody understands what is being asked and how it is being answered.

A question may be based on a false assumption or facts that you do not accept: 'As the mother has left her violent partner, your concerns about the children witnessing domestic violence no longer apply?' You need to hold on to your case and be sure that you don't give the impression that you have accepted the premise of the question: 'I don't accept that the separation is genuine', or 'This is a very recent development and we would need to be sure that it is sustained'.

Don't guess at an answer

If you are not sure of an answer, say so. If you are asked about a date or asked a question about a number that you are not completely sure about, either make it very clear that you are giving an approximation or say that you are not sure and check the answer in your file. If you are asked, 'How many times did you try to visit?' and guess confidently at 'Four', the lawyer can make you look unreliable by showing that it was only three times. If your answer was, 'I think it was about four times, but I would need to check the file to be sure', the lawyer will either have to give you the chance to check the file, or concede that the exact number isn't really important.

If you don't know the answer to a question, it is acceptable to say so. You are there to give evidence of the facts that you know and to share your professional opinion and analysis of the facts. You are not expected to know everything, and you might be asked to give opinions that are outside your area of professional expertise. If this happens, it is better to be clear and open and say that you don't know, or that you don't have the expertise to give an opinion, than to guess at an answer just for something to say. For example, if you are asked about a parent's mental health, you may not be qualified to give a diagnosis, and should not feel pushed to give one. You should not say that you thought that the mother was suffering from depression, as that would be a medical diagnosis, but you can describe what you saw of her mood – flat, withdrawn, etc.

Say what you want to say, not what the lawyers are trying to make you say

Lawyers are not allowed to ask leading questions in Examination in Chief. A leading question is one which points to the answer, so they cannot ask you, 'Do you think that the children are frightened of their father?', because it will be clear that they want the answer 'Yes'. Instead, they will ask you an open question, for example, 'What is your impression of the children's relationship with their father?' This allows you to say what you want to say.

In cross-examination, the lawyers are allowed to ask leading questions and will want to get you to give answers that support their case. They may ask, 'Is it fair to say that when the mother hasn't been drinking she provides a good standard of care to the children?' Your answer might be, 'Yes, but she hasn't been sober in six months', but you might not be able to get any further than 'Yes…' before the lawyer moves on to their next question, having got the answer that they want. If you start with the qualifying part of your answer, they will have to let you give your whole answer. You might say, 'But she hasn't been able to stop drinking in the last six months, so we can't say what her care of the children would be like now if she wasn't drinking. In the past she has been able to care for them properly.' This would be a full and fair answer.

If you are faced with a lawyer who really won't let you make your points, or whose cross-examination has created a misleading impression, you can try to take some control of your evidence. If your answer is interrupted before you are able to finish it, say that you haven't finished and complete your answer. Either when the lawyer moves on to a different topic, or just at the next question, you can say, 'Before I go on to that issue…' or 'Before I answer that question…', '…I want to make sure that the court is clear about my evidence on the last point', and then say what you need to say. This should not be used too often; if you go back to state minor points or little details you risk looking pedantic and argumentative, but it can be very effective if you have been unable to explain yourself properly.

At the end of your evidence, if you are concerned that an important point has been misunderstood, or that you haven't been as clear on something as you had hoped, you can say so and clear up any misunderstandings. Take paper and pencil into the box with you so that you can scribble a reminder to go back over a point and deal with it at the end of your evidence, which could be hours later.

Don't get drawn into a squabble

Sometimes lawyers will challenge your opinion to try to get you to change it. If there have been new factors that have come out in the course of evidence, it might be possible that you would want to revise your opinion, but this does not usually happen and it is more likely that they are just trying to make you argue with them. If you lose your temper, or get irritated and give a sarcastic answer, you can look less than professional and that impression could colour the rest of your evidence.

Try not to answer a question with a question – 'Yes I did do that, what else could I have done?' – which looks less than confident and invites discussion or argument. If the answer is simply 'Yes' or 'No', that is all that needs to be said.

Bear in mind that lawyers have a duty to put their client's case, and if they are given a completely different version of the facts then they have to raise them with you. If you have described the children as looking dirty during a visit but the parents say that they had just been bathed and dressed in freshly laundered clothes, their lawyer has to put that to you. Depending on how this is done, it can sound like an accusation that you have misled the court. It isn't personal, so don't react as though it is – just assert your version of the facts.

Communicating with your lawyer

It can be quite difficult to hand over responsibility for "your" case to a lawyer to argue, but you do have to be able to let the lawyer do their job. You have to sit quietly in court and possibly listen to parents attack your professionalism, or twist facts to discredit your case. The lawyer will have read your statement and will know what areas need real focus and what issues are not really central to the points that need to be decided in the case.

If the parents concede that they often couldn't get the children to school on time but say that they were only ten minutes late, the lawyer may well decide that that is enough without pushing them to admit that the children were often two hours late. It doesn't help the lawyer if you are whispering instructions from behind them or passing them paper notes stating 'NOT 10 mins, 2hrs!'. Check with your lawyer beforehand whether they are happy to be passed notes; some don't want to be distracted during a line of questioning and will prefer to turn to you at the end of their questioning, or after one area has been dealt with, and check whether you think that anything has been missed. Take a note if the witness says anything new or different, especially if they contradict anything that they have said before. If there is something important that you don't feel that the lawyer has dealt with, tell them at the time. Lawyers only get one chance to question witnesses, so if something is missed, you need to tell them there and then.

Once you are in the witness box, your only communication with your lawyer is through the questions that they are asking you. Technically, you are not allowed to speak to them during breaks in your evidence, so you can expect to be lunching alone. Sometimes the lawyers will ask the court if this rule can be waived so that you can sort out other matters on the case, or simply to be sociable, but if this is done you must not discuss your evidence with the lawyer or with any other member of your team at court. Once your evidence is finished, the lawyer will usually ask if you can be released, which means that you can either return to sitting with your team or leave court.

TIP 9

Don't just leave court afterwards...

Don't just leave court after the hearing – there will probably be some points you need to consider first.

Make sure you understand exactly what decision has been made

It can sometimes be surprisingly difficult to follow exactly what has been decided; sometimes the judge will indicate which approach to an issue she prefers and leave the lawyers to draft the detailed order on that basis. Sometimes different parts of an order can be indicated in different places in the judgment and you need to make sure that you have picked up on everything.

Keep a note of what order you think has been made and check it against your lawyer's note.

Get a copy of the order if available, or a draft from your lawyer

Courts vary in how they will produce their orders. Some court clerks will be typing up the order as the judge reads it out and will be able to give you copies soon after you leave court. Sometimes judges will leave details of an order to be agreed between the lawyers. A judge might ask the lawyers to draw up the order and bring it back for his approval. An order might be for another hearing 'on the first open date after…' and the lawyers may have to go to the court list office to establish what date is available before completing the order.

Make a note of relevant dates

An interim court order will usually set out the timetable for the next steps in the case. Make sure that you have noted the date of the next hearing, the date on which you will next be required to file a statement, report or care plan, and the dates of any actions that need to be taken, meetings convened, contact arranged, etc. If you haven't been given a copy of the order, it may take several days, or possibly weeks, before the order is typed up and signed by the judge. Timetables are often tight and if you wait for an order to be produced formally and sent to you, you may miss several significant deadlines.

Does anything need to be done immediately?

If an interim care order or emergency protection order has just been made, you will need to make practical arrangements to implement it. Get copies of the order to show the police and any carers from whom you are going to remove the child; warn the foster carers that the child will be arriving and give them a copy of the order in case the parents challenge them; and set in motion the practical arrangements for bringing the child into local authority care. If appointments need to be set up for an assessment, or for contact, as a result of the order, try to get them set up by phone while everybody is still at court and the parents have the benefit of their lawyer present.

If the decision went against you

Ask your lawyer if there are any grounds for appeal. Appeals are not
granted automatically, but only if the court made a decision that no
reasonable court, properly directed, could have made. Courts have a
wide discretion in children and family cases and you cannot appeal a
decision just because you think that it is wrong. There are tight
deadlines for appeals, so you will need to find out immediately if there
are any grounds and start considering whether or not you will be
appealing the decision. If you are going to appeal, you will also need
to decide whether you need to apply for a stay of execution –
preventing any action being taken on an order until the appeal has
been heard. If you do not apply for a stay, the order will be valid from
the moment that it is made and you will be required to implement it.

TIP 10

Know what actions you should take after court

Tell the child

The child, if they are old enough to know that the case has been in court, and their carers will need to know what has been decided and what that means for them. Will the child be moved or stay with their current carers; are there any changes to contact; will they be seeing somebody for assessment; and when is the next hearing?

Inform the people who need to implement the order

Wherever possible, send copies of the order to the professionals needed to put the order into effect. Your manager may need to authorise funding; the family placement team may need to provide or retain a foster placement; the police may need to support the removal of the child.

If a decision has been made about an assessment, make sure that the relevant expert knows that they will be required to carry out the assessment. It is not unheard of for an expert to give a timetable or have detailed discussions about how an assessment is to be carried out, but then not have their instructions confirmed for a week or so after the hearing, by which time you may have lost the proposed appointments.

If the hearing has been a final hearing and a care plan for adoption has been approved, the parents must be offered counselling and specialist adoption support. Many local authorities have an external provider for these services as birth parents are more likely to take up services that are not connected to the social workers involved in care proceedings.

Update the child's status on your electronic systems

Systems should be updated as soon as possible. The time immediately after a hearing can be one of high anxiety for the parents: their child may have been removed, or they may have been expecting her return, or they may react impulsively or aggressively to an unexpected result. If something happens out of hours or when you are not available, other workers need to be able to see immediately what the child's current legal status is and what happened in court.

Book dates for panels, medicals, planning meetings, etc, that will need to be ready for the next hearing

As well as all the necessary bureaucracy surrounding a child becoming a looked after child for the first time, you will need to work backwards from the dates fixed in the order and make sure that they will be met. You may need to file a care plan in a month's time, but if that plan is for adoption you will need an agency decision that the child should be placed for adoption, which needs a Child's Permanence Report, which needs a medical report, and so on. There is considerable pressure on courts to get proceedings dealt with as quickly as possible and timescales are usually very tight.

If you are considering an appeal

Ask your legal department to request an advice on the merits of an appeal from the lawyer who conducted the hearing. Alert your managers to the possibility of an appeal and find out who within your organisation would have to authorise an application to appeal. Appeals can be expensive, and can cause significant delay for the child. There may be political and practical reasons why a local authority would choose not to pursue an appeal even if there was a reasonable chance of success.

If an appeal is to be considered, the decision to appeal must be taken quickly. Check with your legal department about the time limits on an appeal in the specific circumstances; they are usually very tight, sometimes as little as 14 days, and if you miss a deadline there will need to be a separate application for permission to bring an appeal out of time.

Continue to work with the family

One of the hardest parts about taking a case to court is that you will almost certainly need to continue to work with the child's family, whatever the result. If your court application is successful, they will possibly see you as having betrayed any positive relationship that they had established with you; while if they have a judgement in their favour, however minor, they may take the decision as invalidating all of your concerns and be unable to see any need to co-operate any further with you or the local authority.

Adoption cases

An adoption order should not be made without the adopters and child present, which can cause a difficulty as the birth parents are entitled to be given notice of the final adoption hearing. Courts get around this by listing the hearing in two parts:

- the formal part, where the actual decision is made and which the birth parents may attend and where evidence may be heard; and
- a "celebration hearing".

The celebration will be fixed for the adopters and child only, at least 14 days after the final hearing. This is after the time allowed for the birth parents to appeal has expired. The celebration is an informal event, at which the judge signs the final order, meets the child and allows photographs to be taken in court. Social workers may attend the celebration to support the family.

Start preparing for the next hearing!

References

Bar Standards Board (2014) *The Bar Standards Board Handbook*, London: Bar Standards Board

CAFCASS (2014) *Care Applications in March 2014*, available at: www.cafcass.gov.uk/news/2014/april/march-2014-care-demand-statistics.aspx

Department for Education (2013) *Working Together to Safeguard Children: A guide to inter-agency working to safeguard and promote the welfare of children*, London: Department for Education, available at: www.gov.uk/government/publications/working-together-to-safeguard-children

Department for Education (2014) *Statutory Guidance on Court Orders and Pre-Proceedings for Local Authorities*, London: Department for Education, available at: www.gov.uk/government/uploads/system/uploads/attachment_data/file/281452/Statutory_Guidance_on_court_orders_and_pre-proceedings_18.2.pdf

Family Rights Group (2012) *Family Group Conferences*, accessed at: www.frg.org.uk/involving-families/family-group-conferences

Judiciary of England and Wales (2010) *Guidelines for Judges Meeting Children who are Subject to Family Proceedings*, available at: www.judiciary.gov.uk/JCO%2fDocuments%2fFJC%2fvoc%2fGuidelines_+Judges_seeing_+Children.pdf

Ministry of Justice (2013) *International Child Abduction and Contact Unit*, available at: www.justice.gov.uk/protecting-the-vulnerable/

official-solicitor/international-child-abduction-and-contact-unit

Ministry of Justice (2014a) *Practice Direction 12A: Care, supervision and other Part 4 proceedings: guide to case management*, available at: www.justice.gov.uk/downloads/protecting-the-vulnerable/care-proceeding-reform/pd12a.pdf

Ministry of Justice (2014b) *The Public Law Outline: Guide to case management in public law proceedings*, London: Ministry of Justice

Useful resources

https://courttribunalfinder.service.gov.uk//
A court service website giving addresses of courts and tribunals in England and Wales.

www.gov.uk/government/uploads/system/uploads/attachment_data/file/281452/Statutory_Guidance_on_court_orders_and_pre-proceedings_18.2.pdf
Department for Education Statutory Guidance on Court Orders and Pre-Proceedings, for local authorities (published April 2014).

http://hmctsformfinder.justice.gov.uk/HMCTS/FormFinder.do
HM Courts and Tribunals Service website, which provides a range of forms and explanatory leaflets about court services.

www.bailii.org/
British and Irish Legal Information Institute (BAILII) website, which provides free transcripts of court judgements from the UK and Europe.

www.gov.uk/government/publications/cross-border-child-protection-cases-the-1996-hague-convention
Department for Education Statutory Guidance on how to deal with childcare cases involving an international element.

www.justice.gov.uk/downloads/protecting-the-vulnerable/care-proceeding-reform/public-law-outline-flowchart.pdf
Ministry of Justice-produced flowchart which shows the different stages and timescales involved in the Public Law Outline.

www.cafcass.gov.uk/leaflets-resources.aspx
Children and Family Court Advisory and Support Service (CAFCASS)
website, which provides leaflets and videos for adults and children to
support legal work involving family breakdown, adoption, domestic
violence and a range of other subjects.

Glossary

Appeal

Application to a higher court to overturn the decision of a lower court. An appeal can only be considered if the lower court has made an error of law or fact, and not simply used in an attempt to get a different decision from the court.

Bench

The judges or magistrates hearing a case, also the physical place in which they sit.

Child arrangements order

Applicable to England and Wales. A court order under Section 8 of the Children Act 1989 (as amended by the Children and Families Act 2014) regulating with whom a child is to live, spend time or otherwise have contact, and when.

Child assessment order

An order under section 43 of the Children Act 1989 or article 62 of the Children (Northern Ireland) Order 1995 which gives a local authority or authorised person the right to carry out an assessment of a child whom they suspect may be at risk. The order must include a start and finish date, with a maximum active period of seven days.

Children's Guardian/Guardian ad Litem

A Children's Guardian (in England and Wales, Guardian ad Litem in Northern Ireland) is appointed in care and related proceedings to represent the child's interests and to assist the court in reaching a decision in the best interests of the child. They are qualified social workers, independent from the local authority and work with an independent solicitor representing the child.

Chronology

A complete history, in date order, of the child and of the family if relevant. A good chronology can create a clear factual picture of the family and present a lot of information in a concise and easy to follow format.

Contact Activity Direction

Applicable to England and Wales. An order under section 11A of the Children Act 1989 which requires a party to undertake an activity, e.g. classes or counselling, which would support and facilitate their contact with a child.

Contact order

An order under section 8 of the Children Act 1989 or article 8 of the Children (Northern Ireland) Order 1995 requiring a person with whom the child lives to permit the child to have contact with the person named in the order. This has now been superseded in England and Wales by child arrangements orders.

Counsel

The barrister representing a party in court. In the most serious cases, a party may have a senior barrister, known as Queen's Counsel, QC, or "silk" (named after the fabric of their robes).

County court

Court dealing with a wide range of civil (i.e. non-criminal) matters, including all family matters and care proceedings. Since April 2014, county courts have been part of the unified Family Court in England and Wales.

Court clerk/court legal adviser

A qualified solicitor or barrister who sits with lay magistrates and advises them on the law and procedure. In the higher courts where the judges are legally qualified, the court clerk plays an administrative and support role and does not give advice.

Court of Appeal

A court in England and Wales, and in Northern Ireland, which has a Criminal and a Civil Division. The Civil Division hears appeals from family courts. Leave to appeal has to be granted by a single judge before the full court of three judges hears the substantive appeal. It sits at the Royal Courts of Justice in London or Belfast, and occasionally in other large court centres in England and Wales.

District judge

Junior judges in the Family Court, also district judges (in a magistrates' court) who sit as legally qualified magistrates. They should be addressed as 'Sir' or 'Madam'.

Emergency protection order

An order under section 44 of the Children Act 1989 or article 62 of the Children (Northern Ireland) Order 1995 allowing the local authority to take a child into accommodation or to prevent his or her removal from a safe place. It lasts for eight days, and can be renewed once only for a further seven days.

European Court of Human Rights

Court attached to the Council of Europe (not the EU), which hears complaints that states or state bodies have breached the European Convention on Human Rights. Application can only be made once all domestic avenues have been exhausted.

Family court

In April 2014, all family courts in England and Wales were unified as the Family Court, enabling cases to be brought and heard in one place, rather than being transferred between different tiers of the court system.

Family proceedings court

Magistrates' courts where most care proceedings are started and where the most straightforward cases are dealt with. Since April 2014, they have been part of the unified Family Court in England and Wales.

Freeing order

An order under articles 17 or 18 of the Adoption (Northern Ireland) Order 1987, and under the Adoption Act 1976 in England and Wales pre-2005, which removes all parental responsibility from the parent of a child and gives sole parental responsibility to the adoption agency. The child's parents become known as "former parents" and have no legal relationship with the child.

Guardian ad Litem
See Children's Guardian.

High Court
Court dealing with more complex cases. It is divided into several divisions. The Family Division has now been absorbed into the unified Family Court in England and Wales, but retains a separate identity to exercise inherent jurisdiction.

Inherent jurisdiction
Wide-ranging powers of the High Court to make orders about the care of vulnerable adults and children. Some examples of typical use are to make decisions about medical treatment for seriously ill children, or to recover children from other countries.

Injunction
An order either preventing a person from carrying out an action, or requiring a person to carry out a specific action. Typical uses are non-molestation or occupation orders to protect victims of domestic violence.

Judicial review
The High Court (Administrative Division) can be asked to look at decisions made by public bodies and consider whether the decision has been made reasonably, fairly and properly. After a judicial review, the court can either require the public body to make the decision again or substitute their own decision.

Letter before proceedings
In England and Wales, the local authority issues a letter before proceedings when they are contemplating applying to court. This is a trigger for the Legal Services Commission to allow access to funding for independent legal advice, which is not available while a child is subject only to a child protection plan. This letter will set out clearly the difficulties that the local authority has identified and what the family has to do to avoid proceedings.

Magistrate
A person with no legal qualifications who sits with others, usually a group of three, to hear the least complicated care cases.

Official Solicitor (OS)

The Official Solicitor (OS) is a department of the Ministry of Justice which acts as a litigation friend for vulnerable persons who lack capacity to conduct proceedings. If the OS acts for a parent in care proceedings, a civil servant will act for the parent, but will also instruct a solicitor to represent them.

Parental responsibility agreement

A father without parental responsibility or a step-parent can acquire parental responsibility for a child through formal agreement with every other person who has parental responsibility for that child. The agreement must be made on the correct form and registered with the court to be effective.

Party

Persons or organisations, e.g. local authorities, who are directly involved in proceedings. Other people, e.g. grandparents, can apply to be part of the proceedings by being *joined* as a party or by being permitted to attend hearings as observers without being parties.

Placement order

Applicable to England and Wales. An order under section 21 of the Adoption and Children Act 2002 authorising a local authority to place a child for adoption with any prospective adopters who may be chosen by the authority. It continues in force until it is revoked, or an adoption order is made in respect of the child, or the child marries, forms a civil partnership or attains the age of 18. Only local authorities may apply for placement orders.

Police protection

Not an order, but a power under section 46 of the Children Act 1989 or article 65 of the Children (Northern Ireland) Order 1995 for a police officer to remove a child if there is reasonable cause to believe that the child would otherwise suffer significant harm. The child must be taken to local authority accommodation as soon as possible and may only be kept in police protection for a maximum of 72 hours.

Private Law

Law governing relationships between individuals, e.g. adoption, where one individual is taking over another individual's parental rights.

Public Law

Law governing relationships between individuals and the state, e.g. care proceedings, where a local authority intervenes in a family's life.

Recovery order

An order under section 50 of the Children Act 1989 and article 69 of the Children (Northern Ireland) Order 1995 made when a child has been abducted from care. It requires any person to produce the child or disclose any information he or she has as to the child's whereabouts.

Residence order

An order under section 8 of the Children Act 1989 or article 8 of the Children (Northern Ireland) Order 1995 declaring with whom a child should live. This has now been superseded in England and Wales by child arrangements orders.

Seek and find order

Order of the High Court under the inherent jurisdiction directing the Tipstaff to locate and recover a child.

Special guardianship order

Applicable to England and Wales. An order under section 14A of the Children Act 1989, giving parental responsibility to a person (other than a child's parent), and allowing them to use their parental responsibility to the exclusion of any other person with parental responsibility for that child.

Specific issue order

An order under section 8 of the Children Act 1989 or article 8 of the Children (Northern Ireland) Order 1995 which decides a particular question in relation to a child, e.g. where a child should go to school, or a change of name.

Supreme Court

Formerly known as the House of Lords. The highest appellate court, which hears appeals from all four countries of the UK on significant points of law only.

Tipstaff

An officer of the High Court who can exercise the High Court's powers. He or she has the power to force an entry to property, to make arrests and to commandeer police officers to assist him or her. The Tipstaff is most commonly used to trace and recover children abducted from care or from a parent.

Undertakings

Promises made to the court as part of or as an alternative to court orders. Breach of an undertaking is punishable as contempt of court, which could involve committal to prison.

Usher

A member of court staff who makes sure that the court day runs smoothly. Their job is to make sure that everyone is in the right place at the right time. They are useful sources of information about the practicalities of the court building.

Wardship

An order of the High Court as part of the inherent jurisdiction which gives custody of the child to the High Court. The child may be placed with a local authority or an individual, but all decisions about the child must be made by the court. Wardship can only be used if the issues cannot be resolved under the Children Act.

Orders and section/article numbers

Often, orders are referred to by the number of the section of the Children Act (or, in Northern Ireland, the number of the article of the Children Order) under which they were made rather than by name, and knowing to which orders each section/article refers can help follow discussions at court. Some of the orders most often referred to in this way are outlined below.

Section 8/article 8

Orders under section 8 of the Children Act 1989 or article 8 of the Children (Northern Ireland) Order. These include residence orders, contact orders, child arrangements orders, specific issue orders and prohibited steps orders. Section 8 orders cannot be made in respect of a child who is in the care of a local authority, except for a residence order which will bring the care order to an end.

Section 20 accommodation/article 21

The provision of accommodation for a child by a local authority without a court order. The child can be removed from the accommodation by a parent at any time and the local authority does not have any parental responsibility for the child.

Section 31/article 50

A care order, giving parental responsibility to a local authority and restricting the ability of a parent to exercise their own parental responsibility.

Section 34(4)/article 53(4)

An order allowing a local authority to refuse contact between a child and a parent. Without an order, the local authority has a duty to allow the parent and child reasonable contact.

Section 38(6)/article 57(6)

When a court makes an interim care or supervision order, it may also make directions about the assessment of a child. This was originally intended to prevent unnecessary assessment, but its use has expanded to order local authorities to arrange a residential assessment or to place a child with potential carers for assessment.

Schedule 2, para 19/article 33

Making arrangements for a child looked after by a local authority to live overseas, which requires the consent of all parents for an accommodated child, or the court's permission for a child in care.